Commissioned by Robert Madeson for The Dillingham Arts Council, D ... *2009*

The Last Fr

Score

1. Sunrise at Denali

Kenneth D. Friedrich

16
Euph.
Pno.
mf
20
mf
23
mp

Euph.
Pno.
25
27
31
p

Piu Mosso
35
Euph.
mf
3
35
Pno.
mp
39
Euph.
3
39
Pno.
43
Euph.
43
Pno.

47
Euph.
Pno.
50
f
53

Euph.
Pno.
Adagio ♩= 52
mp
Ped.

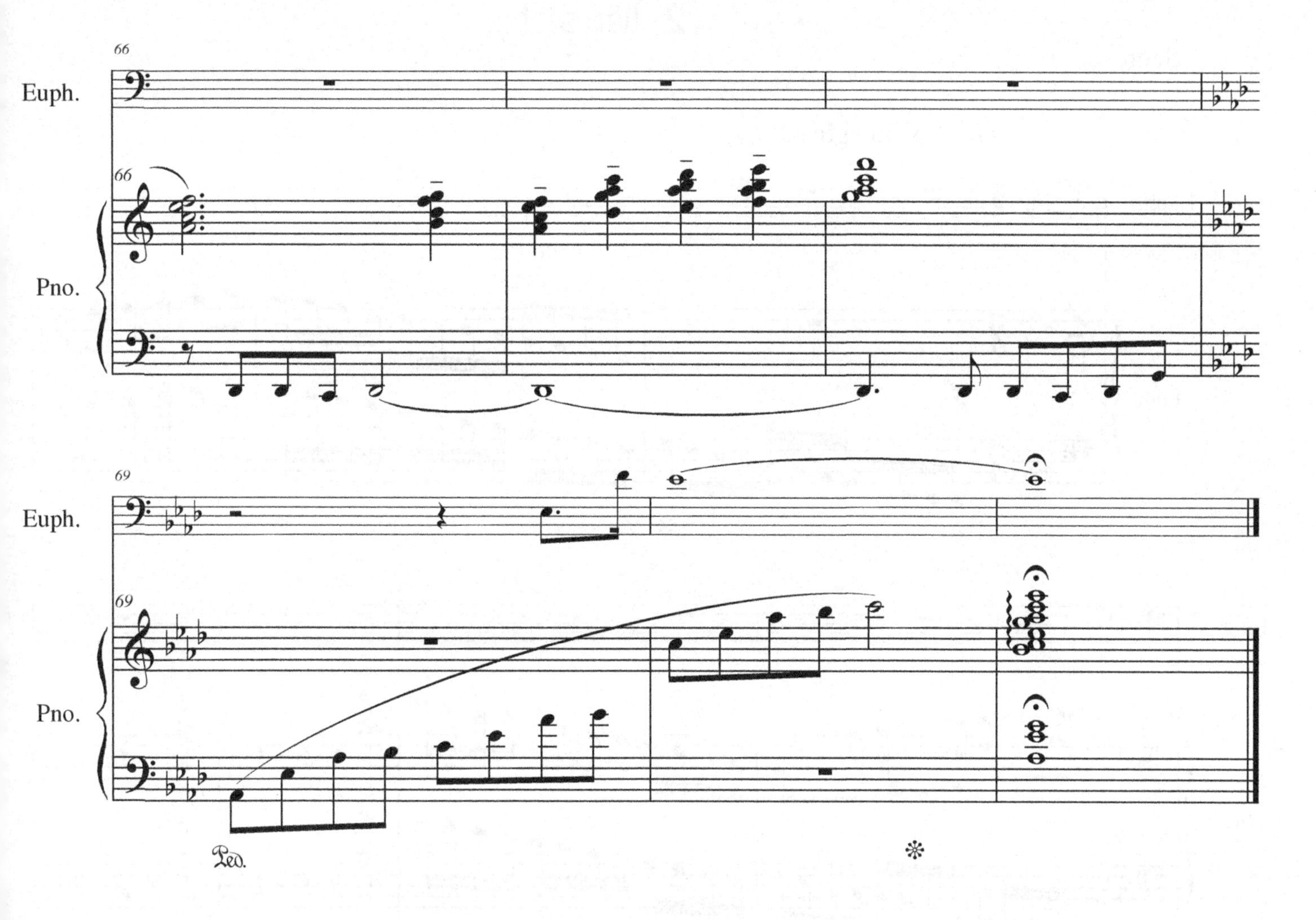
66
Euph.
Pno.
69
Euph.
Pno.

2. Mush!

Score

12
Euph.
Pno.
ff
16
20
f

25
Euph.
Pno.
Allegro Scherzo
30
mp
34
mf

Euph.
Pno.
Euph.
Pno.
Euph.
Pno.

50
Euph.
Pno.
54
58
1.
ff

62
Euph.
2.
f
Pno.
ff
68
73
3

78
Euph.
Pno.
82
Euph.
f
ff
Pno.
ff

3. Arctic Dream

Score

Arctic Dream

19
Euph.
2
19
Pno.
Ped.
22
Euph.
22
Pno.
Ped.
25
Euph.
mf
25
Pno.
Ped.

Euph.
Pno.
Euph.
Pno.
Euph.
Pno.

Arctic Dream

46
Euph.
f
46
Pno.
mp
Ped.
Ped.
49
Euph.
49
Pno.
Ped.
52
Euph.
52
Pno.

54
Euph.
Pno.
57
rit.
mp
♩. = 60
59
mp
Ped.
* Ped.

62
Euph.
p
62
Pno.
p
Ped.
65
Euph.
65
Pno.
Ped.
Ped.
68
Euph.
68
Pno.
Ped.

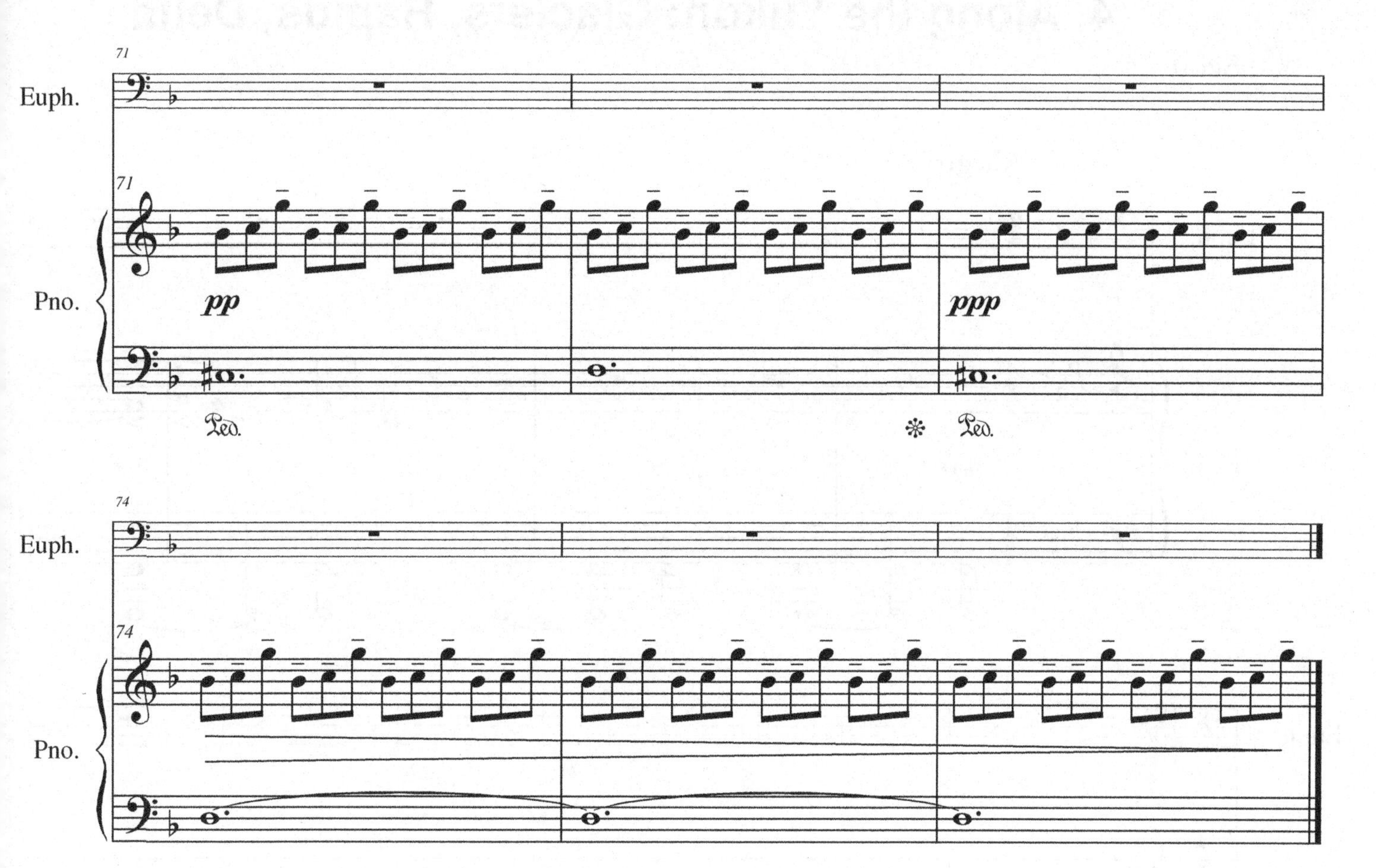
71
Euph.
Pno.
pp
ppp
Ped.
Ped.
74
Euph.
Pno.

4. Along the Yukon: Glaciers, Rapids, Delta

Score

19
uph.
19
Pno.
25
uph.
25
3
Pno.
31
uph.
31
Pno.

Euph.
Pno.
mf

45
Euph.
Pno.
48
Euph.
Pno.
51
Euph.
f
Pno.

54
Euph.
3
3
54
Pno.
57
Euph.
57
Pno.
60
Euph.
60
Pno.

63
uph.
63
Pno.
3
67
uph.
67
Pno.
Animato
71
uph.
71
Pno.
f

75
Euph.
Pno.
79
83
1. meno mosso
mp
3

Euph.
Pno.
rit.
Ped.
2. a tempo
2.
rit.
a tempo
a tempo

98
Euph.
Pno.
101
1.
104

uph.
Pno.
ff
ff

116
Euph.
116
Pno.
119
Euph.
meno mosso
mf
3
119
Pno.
mp
123
Euph.
3
3
123
Pno.

Tempo assai
127
Euph.
3
127
Pno.
mp
Ped.
132
Euph.
132
Pno.
136
Euph.
136
Pno.

140
Euph.
140
Pno.
143
Euph.
143
Pno.
f
147
Euph.
147
Pno.

uph.
Pno.
mf
3

163
Euph.
163
Pno.
167
Euph.
167
Pno.
171
Euph.
171
Pno.

174
Euph.
174
Pno.
177
Euph.
177
Pno.
180
Euph.
180
Pno.

Allegro ♩= 120
183
Euph.
Pno.
3
187
191

196
uph.
Pno.
200
uph.
Pno.
204
uph.
Pno.

The Last Frontier

Euphonium

1. Sunrise at Denali

Kenneth D. Friedrich

2. Mush!

3. Arctic Dream

Arctic Dream

4. Along the Yukon: Glaciers, Rapids, Delta

Along the Yukon

Allegro ♩ = 120

Made in the USA
Coppell, TX
04 December 2024